BEI GRIN MACHT SICH IHR WISSEN BEZAHLT

- Wir veröffentlichen Ihre Hausarbeit,
  Bachelor- und Masterarbeit

- Ihr eigenes eBook und Buch -
  weltweit in allen wichtigen Shops

- Verdienen Sie an jedem Verkauf

Jetzt bei www.GRIN.com hochladen und kostenlos publizieren

Analysis of the BEM Code of Professional Guidelines

Bandar Hezam

Bibliografische Information der Deutschen Nationalbibliothek:

Die Deutsche Nationalbibliothek verzeichnet diese Publikation in der Deutschen Nationalbibliografie; detaillierte bibliografische Daten sind im Internet über http://dnb.d-nb.de abrufbar.

ISBN: 9783346805959
Dieses Buch ist auch als E-Book erhältlich.

© GRIN Publishing GmbH
Nymphenburger Straße 86
80636 München

Alle Rechte vorbehalten

Druck und Bindung: Books on Demand GmbH, Norderstedt Germany
Gedruckt auf säurefreiem Papier aus verantwortungsvollen Quellen

Das vorliegende Werk wurde sorgfältig erarbeitet. Dennoch übernehmen Autoren und Verlag für die Richtigkeit von Angaben, Hinweisen, Links und Ratschlägen sowie eventuelle Druckfehler keine Haftung.

Das Buch bei GRIN: https://www.grin.com/document/1321036

ASIA PACIFIC UNIVERSITY
TECHNOLOGY & INNOVATION

TITLE	EXAMINE, ANALYZE AND APPLY THE ETHICAL THEORIES AND BEM CODES
NAME	BANDAR NAJI ALI HEZAM
DATE	13/09/2021

TABLE OF CONTENTS

CHAPTER 1

INTRODUCTION TO THE STUDY

1.1   Introduction

A set of moral concepts or systems are referred to as ethics. Ethics is a product of society just as the ideology of many individuals. Generally speaking, engineering ethics is an extremely important part of an engineer. Applicable ethics are the disciplines of engineering ethics that focus on decisions and behaviours of engineers and the consequences of these actions and judgements individually and collectively. There is an area of education and research (Van De Poel 2015). Engineering ethics is vital if an engineer can assess each scenario and problem in view of the many elements involved in decision-making that otherwise may lead to non-favourable outcomes without ethical consideration. With regard to engineering ethics, it is far more than simply preventing unlawful technical operations. It's also about ensuring that the customer or user of the product of an engineer is safeguarded against ineptitude and is at the forefront of the engineer's thinking, because a small error or a lack of ethics may endanger many lives.

Briefly, the safety of people should be the first priority for every engineer. For instance, a pulled elevator system consisting of lower-resistance cables, an automatic rail system failing, a poorly functioning medical device and a power station emanating radiation and environmental pollution can be life-threatening if a bridge or a facility is built with low-cost materials to reduce costs. Therefore, engineers must always pay precedence to ethical considerations in the simplest designs and methods in order to avoid harming people, society and the environment in any way.

In addition to safety, engineering ethics also plays a critical role in integrity and honesty, as this ethical value guarantees that the professional may operate honestly and openly and without external stress or partiality. It also guarantees that engineers are accountable for their actions, recognising and accepting the individual commitment to the customer and the work. Unless a basic study of engineering ethics has been completed, researchers Harun et al. (2016) have shown that dubious actions can take place, including corruption, bribery, abuse of authority, discrimination and exploitative working practises.

Therefore, it is necessary to understand engineering ethics. It builds up and teaches an engineer to provide priority, in terms of safety, environmental consideration, health and social goods, to the greater benefit of the public (Sahin, 2016). Therefore, the function of ethics in engineering is essential as it depends on the integrity of engineering. The notion that ethics should not be included into technology is too high a risk. The very nature of the life of the people for greater good who suffer from unfair hardship and tough living situations may be upgraded only by ethical engineering techniques. Furthermore, professionals with expert know-how are superior to their customers, employers and the public. An awakened and honest engineer with this knowledge will become a valued member of society. An engineer of ethics therefore damages reputations of engineering, reduces public confidence and becomes a dangerous member of the community. In general, engineering morality may affect life and death, prevent engineers from abusing the public, minimise the danger of accidents in every scenario of engineering, and prevent the creation or use of hazardous technologies and materials.

1.2 Objective

The objective of this assignment is to examine, analyze and apply the ethical theories and the BEM (Board of Engineers Malaysia) Code of Professional Conduct to solve ethical related issues in the practice of engineering.

1.3 Scenario

The RBS plant in Prai Free Trade Zone, Penang, has performed a compliance audit for 5 days (11th to 15th January 2021). This audit was conducted using fifteen man-days. The audit was carried out according to the Customer Code of Conduct standards, local legislation and regulations.

For Disney client, RBS makes goods. It had 4,500 direct workers, and around 3,000 of them foreign workers from various nationalities. The personnel data and records were examined and an onsite audit was done for three months (October, November and December 2020).

The audit lists the following findings:

1. Workers worked over 60 hours a week at the plant.

2. An average of 8% of working people worked twelve days in a month in a row.

3. For employees, the plant had no work hours and rest days monitoring policy or method.

4. The job without LOTO (Lock Out Tag Out) security control was detected during the in-house audit –

  A. Contractors operating the electrical cables installation and maintenance in a plant.

  B. Workers in the restricted area of the pump had no certified work permit.

  C. Space restricted has not been recognized.

  D. For the usage in the waste chemistry area, expansion power cables were found.

5. The plant was obligated to offer foreign workers with accommodation. The apartment was in a residential neighborhood. A smoking was detected in their bed in the dormitory audit –

  A. Workers in 2 of the residences.

  B. 3 room fans without cover have been found.

  C. The cooking area was filled with insects (rodents and ants).

  D. In the women's dormitory a male warden was found on the site.

CHAPTER 2

LITERATURE REVIEW

2.1 Introduction

A standard exists in each engineering company that all the members should comply with, commit and apply. In general, no specific right or wrong option exists for each ethical circumstance, therefore engineers need to provide guidelines, framework or reference in order to comprehend their duties. These principles are structured into a defined set of codes known as the Code of Conduct. In line with applicable laws, regulations, rules and the highest standards of ethics and values, the Code of Conduct is intended by the complete person. It gives a framework for an ethical assessment for the worker, outlines the rights, duties, obligations of members. For companies, shareholders and other stakeholders, the topics covered in this code are of paramount importance. This Code shall enter into force as soon as possible. It shall be the obligation of all members to obey the terms of this code in spirit and in writing by a corporation or an organization practicing the Code of Conduct. To this day, many businesses use the Code of Conduct in Malaysia and the Malaysia engineering board more in context (BEM).

2.2 BEM Code of Professional Guidelines

According to the code no. 1.1.2 which clearly states that an engineer shall be hold accountable for his/her signature on any approvals or important documents related to projects. So as a professional engineer he/she must be well aware of the situation and understand before giving approvals to any project and signing documents off. This can be applied to the situation as the engineers can cross-check the documents and avoid open-handed approvals to projects or work that are unethical and may cause injury or harm the safety of the public.

Code no. 1.1.3 states that, a professional practicing engineer shall respond by informing the relevant authorities about any on-going ethical issues or problem within a reasonable period of time. It is necessary for the engineer to obtain a written notification within appropriate time, which would enable the board to set up a panel that may eliminate the issue. Failure to do so may imply incompetence on the part of being an ethical engineer, which would warrant retribution. Regardless of the severity

6

of the problem, it is vital that the board is alerted and that steps are taken to avoid further inconveniences that may occur in the future.

Code no. 1.1.4 means that a Practicing Professional Engineer shall undertake projects only if he is qualified by education and experience in the specific technical fields of that project. The engineer with the certificate of practice cannot be considered as qualified by education alone, an experience is also required to determine whether the person is qualified for the job or oversight. For example, when a freshly graduated engineer is enrolled with the BEM, he / she picks a particular area of interest for the professional career to be pursued. If for any reason he / she chooses to deviate or move from the particular field of interest, the board has to be informed. Failure to do this can result in the being penalized or prohibited to practice as an engineer meaning, the license can be revoked by the board.

BEM Code 1.1.7 emphasizes on integrity and faithfulness, it states that a qualified engineer shall always act in an unbiased and truthful manner while composing papers, comments and testimonies. The details about each initiative shall be associated and modified with the truth and data dependent on the current project. As a qualified engineer, any comment or referral to competent authority on any ethical problem should be reported to and to the supervisor with no direct interest. This proper communication can be beneficial in interest of the public for their safety rather than using the information for personal benefit or advantage.

In 1.1.8 of the BEM Code of Conduct, Professionally practicing engineers must be truthful in presenting certain comments or technical records and should not be supplying the public with any false facts. Moreover, professional engineers should not disclose or publish any technical data or confidential records in the public because they could tarnish their own image as well as that of their clients and employees. Finally, engineers may not include arguments, criticism or statements by third parties unless the actors underlined in the statement are included in the statement.

Code 1.1.10 ensures that the qualified engineer is acquainted with the applicable code of ethics. When any rule is infringed by either employee or colleague; senior or junior, the board should be informed during that time.

Under 1.2.1 of the BEM code, qualified engineers must meet certain technical requirements with regard to the qualifications and code of ethics before applying or certifying the execution of any technical project. For example, all the design requirements stated by the client prior to project approval must be met during the project submission and approval period until the project can be approved as completed, and the project must pass all the safety checks to requires before being authorized of completion and usage.

According to the Code 1.2.2, a qualified engineer is advised that he undertakes all the responsibility for the project before completion, even though the job is finished. This eliminates the blame game particularly where a certain project has been turned off by one engineer to another, it increases the stress of liability and tells the engineer that any adverse consequences arising from the behavior taken at the time of handover. The danger must be borne by the professional engineer and his company.

Code 1.2.3 states that a licensed Professional Engineer with a Certification shall not report past and current evidence, details or knowledge without the prior permission of the Customer or Employer, except as permitted or necessary by statute or when the confidentiality of such knowledge is detrimental to public protection, health and security. The data acquired from the projects or dealings are confidential, which should not be reveled in public as it may affect the life of project along with the position of the engineer and reputation of the company.

Code 1.2.4 outlines the duty of any licensed Registered Engineer with Certification of Practice having knowledge of some violation of this Code of Conduct or of any regulation or rule to report immediately to the Employer or responsible professional bodies. If necessary, also inform to public authorities and cooperate with appropriate authorities in the delivery of such details.

Code 1.2.5 implies that in cases when there is a professional guidance or advice suggested by a Qualified Engineer with relevant qualification ignored, and neglect of his opinion that may jeopardize the safety, welfare and health interest of the public, it is the duty of the engineer to inform his Employer or Company and the relevant authority, describing and justifying the implications of neglect of his professional advice.

BEM Code 1.3.1 states, a licensed Professional Engineer with a Practice Credential shall not receive any financial or other gain or compensation from more than one party for technical engineering services on the same project, unless the circumstances are completely stated and decided upon by all involved parties. For example, acceptance of any sort of rewards rather be financial or in terms of gifts are considered as a bribe if an engineer accepts anything from other parties in exchange for project related services. Furthermore, as a professional engineer, they should not approve or seek contracts from their respective client, directly or indirectly, except with Its employer's knowledge. Ultimately, all technical guidance will be given to their client and employer in a faithful and honest manner, or any engagement of engineering work.

BEM code 1.3.2 says a qualified engineer shall disclose any details or friendship or concern that could affect his judgement in a possible conflicts of interest which may affect or appear to influence his decision or the nature of his services. This is to prevent potential imbalances in its direction and to prevent undermining its function or operation.

2.3 Ethical Theories

Ethical theories form part of the decision-making basis when it comes to ethics since they reflect the points of view from which people seek direction in decision-making. When examining different cultures and communities, human comportment may be divided into ethical and moral theories and can also determine the connectivity of behavioral patterns and notions of the right and wrong.

Ethical theories emphasize several factors, distinct decision-making styles or a different rule of decision, such as foreshadowing your results and following other tasks in order to make an ethically correct option. Not everyone makes the same judgements, uses the same information and uses the same decision-making principles. A shared set of objectives must be grasped for successful decision-makers in order to understand ethical theory further. These include four goals:

1) Relativism
2) Utilitarianism
3) Duty ethics and Right ethics
4) Virtue Ethics

9

2.3.1 Relativism

Ethical relativism is a theory that morality is relative to culture. This is to say, it is based on a community's moral standards in which activity is carried out whether it is good or evil. The same act may be moral in one group, while moral in another. For an ethical relativist there are no universal moral principles that can always be applied worldwide to all peoples. It is their own moral standards that may be evaluated in a community's activities. If ethical relativism is true, a common framework for resolving moral disputes or reaching an agreement on ethical concerns cannot be established among individuals of diverse cultures.

The Theory of ethical relativism is denied by ethicists. Some say that while civilizations' moral practices may be different, they are not based on basic moral principles. For example, it was normal practice to murder parents at a certain age, based on the notion that people were better off after life, as long as they were physically active and energetic. In our society this behavior would be condemned, but we would agree with these societies on the moral principles underpinning the obligation to look after parents. The companies may thus differ, yet agree on the principles in their implementation of core moral values.

Some moral convictions may also be linked with culture while others are not. It is also proposed. Some actions, including attire and decency norms, may be based on local customs while others may be subject to general principles of morality, such as slavery, torture or political repression and may be misunderstood in spite of numerous other cultural variations. Just while some of the practices are relatively distinct, they are not all related. In general, ethics related to one's own culture is generation and time.

2.3.2 Utilitarianism

The usefulness indicates that behavior is desirable or suitable for maximizing social or public wellbeing. It is actually an all-encompassing strategy aimed at maximizing human well-being. The findings are analyzed and the results are seen as correct if they offer advantages that maximize social wellbeing but generate problems for certain persons. For example, building a bridge will help society yet does not have a negative environmental impact.

The train, which is out of control at fast speed towards a crowd, might also be another illustration. A person managing the train now has the option, either to go to

10

another track, or to pull the crowd and endanger the lives of many. Utilitarianism gives priority to the people in this circumstance, and just a single individual would switch to the road. Two distinct types of utilitarianism:

1) Act utilitarianism
2) Rule utilitarianism

Act utilitarianism is the concept applied directly in a situation of choice to each alternative conduct. The correct act is therefore defined as the one that gives most people the best consequences or advantages. Criticisms of this point of view include on the difficulties of achieving full knowledge and of our actions. For example, assume that a person may terminate a regional conflict by torturing children whose dads are enemy soldiers and thereby exposing the fathers' hiding place.

The rule utilitarianism is the concept used to establish the justification of standards of conduct. A regulation such as promise maintenance is established by taking into account the ramifications of an environment that violates promises and makes pledges in a world that has commitments made. The rules to be obeyed or violated are thus termed right and wrong. For example, slavery in Greece can be correct if it leads to a complete achievement for some misuse able people of cultivated bliss.

2.3.3 Duty ethics and Right ethics

The distinction between right and wrong is determined by ethics. Law is laws which have to be observed willingly and unintentionally, whereas ethics is optional. It expects that your rights are respected and that the rights of others are protected via ethical obligations since it ethically is more than complying with legislation.

A law is an expectation or a method of action that is supported by the legal or moral basis of something that you deserve. People have every sort of right, whether legal, moral, spiritual, natural or basic. The right to society's education or to have arms are examples of rights. A series of human rights, animals or societies have to be recognized and respected through ethical action.

The acknowledgment of rights is a direct outcome of duties. Every individual is obliged to uphold or comply with the rights of someone else just as they are obliged to protect your rights. Once a person acknowledges a right or is taught about it, he and others must defend that right. You have the right to freedom of expression, for example,

11

but everyone around you has the same right. You have an obligation to respect his right to speak anything even if someone says that you do not accept. You have the obligation to respect the rights of others and occasionally to protect them.

2.3.4 Virtue Ethics

The concept of virtue ethics highlights the significance of character and virtue in moral philosophy, rather than acting or making good results. Virtue ethics ideas are mostly history-inspired, in that a man of virtue has ideal features. These characteristics come from the inner impulses but must be cultivated. But once they are established, they will be stable. For example, a virtuous person is someone with a lovely character, not because he or she wants to improve its value and achieve benefits in many scenarios. Its ideas give an autonomous understanding of ethics, because the development of humanity is perceived as an aim in its own right and doesn't evaluate properly how far our activities influence others. Virtue ethics also does not offer direction as there are no obvious guiding principles other than that of "doing as a good person in a circumstance would behave." As such, there are no clear guiding principles. Finally, because of education, society, friends, and the family, the capacity to nurture the correct qualities is impacted by several variables outside of a person's control.

2.4 Professional Code & Conduct for Disney

1. Health and Safety (Code 6)

Manufacturers must create a healthy and secure working environment for employees in accordance with all applicable laws and regulations, including appropriate access to clean water, health facilities, fire protection and enough lighting and ventilation. The companies should also ensure that any housing they provide for employees will meet the same cleanliness, health and security standards. (Disney, 2007)

2. Compensation (Code 7)

Disney wants producers to recognise the importance of salaries to satisfy employees' fundamental needs. Manufacturers should follow and give them with statutory advantages, including minimum pay, extra time and the maximum number of hours, portions of the work and other compensatory components, and all existing salary and hour rules and regulations. Companies may not oblige people, if laws do not restrict working hours, to work more than (a) 48 hours weekly plus 12 overtime hours, (b) regular and overtime limitations as provided for by local legislation or (c) working week plus 12 overtime hours. Workers should also be entitled to at least one day off every seven days unless unusual business situations exist. Manufacturers shall recompense employees at an hourly rate of legal compensation or, if legal premium rates are absent, at at least equivalent to the ordinary hours compensation rate. Disney expects manufacturers to fulfil greater requirements if the norms of local industry are superior to the laws in force. (Disney, 2007)

3. Monitoring and Compliance (Code 11)

To guarantee adherence with the Code of Conduct, manufacturers shall allow for unforeseen on-site factory and employer inspections, job book and account assessments, and private interviews with their staff members, together with appointed representatives (including third parties). All documentation required to establish conformity with this Code of Conduct on the site should be kept by the creators. (Disney, 2007)

2.5   Code of Ethics (WFEO)

Code 1.2: *Be objective and truthful*;

Honesty, integrity, continually updated competence, service loyalty and dedication to improve the society's quality of life are the cornerstones of professional responsibility. All available and relevant information on professional reports, reports and testimonies should be unbiased and honest in this respect.(WFEO, 2021)

Code 2.2: *Practise in accordance with accepted engineering practices, standards and codes;*

There are several legal and conformity regulations governing the work you are doing. The compliance rules and / or legislation that you need to comply with for a certain project are essential. This should be mentioned in the letter that also assigns compliance responsibilities. In case of no legislation it may be necessary to create acceptable standards based on internationally recognised sound practise. (WFEO, 2021)

Code 4.1: *Create and implement engineering solutions for a sustainable future;*

Substantial environmental and sustainable development issues have no geographical borders. The sustainability of our economic and social future is not just concerned with the environment but also with the sustainability. No objectives or quotas, only methods. There are nothing. They are not just technology, they are also transitional processes. Eventually, companies can only develop towards sustainability even if management and technology developments are progressive. Consumer behaviour, integrate policy and policy aims, and promote knowledge and capabilities to strengthen protection and restructuring and to promote social and political issues. (WFEO, 2021)

Code 4.2: *Be mindful of the economic, societal and environmental consequences of actions or projects;*

Compliance with the principles of sustainable development will make a major contribution to eradicating poverty in the globe. Sustainability is an ongoing system or process focused on long-term conservation and development integration that brings social and economic benefits, while not jeopardising future generation requirements. Engineers from all countries should be aware of and respect environmental ethics.

CHAPTER 3

ETHICAL PROBLEM ANALYSIS AND DISCUSSION

3.1   Introduction

This chapter analyses the relationship between BEMs, Disney's, and WFEO's professional codes of conduct and ethical theory. The codes and theories are used to assess the topic from a number of angles and to find all possible responses and proper analysis and discussion.

3.2   Analysis & Discussion of the Situation

First, we examine, justify and explain in depth how to combine the BEM's, DOSH's, WFEO's and Disney's professional behavioral codes, which apply particularly to this circumstance, to solve ethical difficulties and to provide adequate advice to the management to handle these problems.

3.2.1   BEM Codes Relating

1.) Code 1.0 of the BEM states quite clearly that the health, safety and welfare of individuals should always be a major concern of an engineer. BEM Code 1.0 is therefore applicable to employees who work more than 60 hours a week in a plant with an average of 8% working 12 consecutive days in a month. This tight schedule puts a lot of pressure on the mental and physical health of workers, which can lead to carelessness, carelessness and many other repercussions, which can jeopardize public safety. In order to remedy this problem, producers must reduce working hours for their employees to a maximum of 48 hours per week with a 12-hour option and pay for overtime. They also need to give a minimum of a day off in a week to prevent them from working consecutively.

The BEM Code 1.0 also includes the safety control on power cabling installation, maintenance, as well as the extension power cables discovered to be utilized in the waste chemical storage area for contracting employees operating without the usage of the LOTO (lock-out tag-out). Without security checks, workers put themselves at serious risk and deaths, since this might lead to an unforeseen accident or limb amputation. Electrocution might happen in the extension power cables in the waste chemical storage area. Therefore, in the interests of resolving this issue,

15

producers should provide the cabling safety control LOTO (Lock Out Tag Out) for workers where they cannot be working and the extensions used in the residue storage area should be installed on walls and properly isolated to ensure no electrocution, by introducing a strict protocol and imposing a heavy penalty.

2.) BEM Code 5.0 stipulates clearly that the engineer is always conducive to the dignity, reputation and usefulness of the profession with an honor, responsibility, ethics and law. Therefore, the BEM Code 5.0 applies for a plant which does not have a policy or method to monitor workers' working times and rest days, personnel operating in the confined space on a pump who do not have an official work permit and a male guard is located at a woman's sleeping lodge. In order for the staff to work so many hours overtime, producers should first of all invested in a suitable time management strategy. Employees should be used to monitor workers' working hours carefully. For workers who do not have an official work permit in the restricted space, producers should ask local authorities for a work authorization and only then allow workers permission to work within the limited space. The manufacturers must use strong action against the male watchdog or charge penalty fees in respect of the male watcher in the female dormitory, because this scenario is contrary to local regulations.

3.) BEM Code 1.5 clearly states that if an engineer's advice is amended and may give rise to a situation that may endanger life and/or property, the engineer must notify his employer or client and such other authority as may be appropriate and explain the consequences to be expected because of his advice being overruled and amended. Therefore, this code applies on the situation where the workers are working for more than 60 hours a week, and 8% of the workers working 12 consecutive days in a month. This situation could result in accidents waiting to happen, putting the safety and health of the public at risk. Hence, the engineers should report this issue to the higher authorities and management since the manufacturers are not paying heed to this concern. Furthermore, this code applies to the workers working without the safety control. The workers should refuse to work without the safety control, as this puts their lives at risk .

4.) Code 4.0 expressly provides for one engineer, for each employer or client, to be trusted agencies or trustees. This Code concerns a dormitory audit which shows that employees live in harmful and unhealthy lives. The manufacturers must treat Disney to provide secure, healthy accommodation for the employees. If violations are committed in this declaration, the creators might be punished severely. The manufacturers must alter the rooms and fix any malfunctioning equipment of any unhealthy and dangerous living conditions in the rooms of any employee.

3.2.2 DOSH's Code of Conduct

1. Code 21 says that the responsibility is to carry out or plan compulsory testing for the purpose of identifying and, as far as practicable, removal or alleviation of the protection or hazard of a product, for any product to be manufactured or supplied at work. This applies when employees work more than 60 hours a week, 8 per cent of employees working twelve consecutive days a month. This code also applies to cases when employees were discovered to work without LOTO security oversight.

2. Code 23 states that if the organizing firm breaches section 21 commits an offence and is subject to a fine of not more than 20,000 ringgit or a sentence of not more than two years in jail, or both.

3. Code 24 provides for every employee who has the obligation to take adequate care of his own safety and health and of other people who may suffer from his or her actions or work failure in the course of any obligation or obligation under this Act or any of its provisions to fulfil the obligation and safety of his or her own employer or individual. If a person is in breach of the provisions of this section, he shall constitute an offence and shall be punishable by no greater than one thousand ringgits or by three months' imprisonment, or both of them if convicted. This Act specifies that every individual at work shall give priority to the health and safety of all those affected. It will also comply with the working and health requirements of OSHA. If this clause is breached, a penalty or a short period behind bars will be applied.

4. Code 32 states that any accident, dangerous incident, workplace contamination, or workplace illness that has happened or is expected to happen at the workplace must be reported to the local occupational safety and health department.

3.2.3 Disney's Code of Conduct

1. Code 6: The sleeping area check indicates that staff smoke on their mattresses in two of their houses. Therefore, personnel were punished for disregarding the situation, which may have resulted in a fire in the rooms, as well as the unprofessional conduct with respect to code 6. This will improve the consciousness of employees and help to keep a working atmosphere across the company. If you wish to smoke, you have to smoke in a smoking zone outside your rooms.

   In the kitchen area, there were also flies and rodents. Fans in 3 rooms were found without protection, since a hand inadvertently may be trapped in it, resulting in severe injury. In order to remedy the problem under Code 6, producers must thus give their employees safe, clean and healthy lodging. If the lodging has been found contaminated by rats and insects, the producers must evacuate the workers promptly and transfer them to a better, clean, healthy lodge. They also need to substitute for any fans without cover.

2. Code 7: Based on the compliance audit, it was found that workers were working in the factory for more than 60 hours per week and an average of 8% of the workers worked twelve days consecutively in a month. Therefore, relating to code 7 to solve the issue, the manufacturers must decrease the working hours to a maximum of 48 hours per week for the workers, with an option of 12 hours overtime and being paid rightfully for the overtime. They must also grant a minimum of a day off in a week, so that they don't work consecutively.

3. Based on code 9 to solve the issue, the manufacturers must follow the local and national laws, rules and regulations while operating. Failure to do so will result in a severe penalty and a breach in the Code of Conduct.

4. In view of Code 11, to resolve the problem, producers should be prepared for unanticipated on-site inspections of production plants and accommodation provided by employers. Book and account assessment will also be done in conjunction with private conversations with employees on employment issues. This removes the possibility of corruption and bribery to increase the organization's authority. Manufacturers must thus constantly exercise safe, healthy and clean working conditions and the ethic of lodging and must not infringe on the Code of Conduct. They must comply with local and national authorities' laws, rules and regulations.

3.2.4 WFEO's Code of Conduct

1. The Code 1.3 suggests to avoid any acts or remarks that may be interpreted as unjustly critical of a colleague or which would favour a colleague's own viewpoint. Following the code the male employee found in the female dormitory is a clear indication that the employee is doing this for his own benefit. Being in the place where they are not supposed to be is a very unethical and unprofessional thing to do as a worker. The employer is authorised to even terminate the contract of the worker.

2. Code 2.2 relates to the manufacturers whose workers were working on an unidentified confined space area without an approved permit, along with the honesty and integrity of the members of the organization in conducting themselves honourably and professionally, eliminating the chance of corruption and bribing to get to higher power withing the organization. This is against the local laws and regulations. To solve the issue, the manufacturers must firstly seek a working permit from the local authorities and only then grant permission to the workers to work on the confined space area. Failure to do so will result in a severe penalty and a breach in the Code of Conduct, adding the firm to a name of violators which is publicly available. Secondly, the organization must conduct unexpected on-site inspections of manufacturing facilities and employer-provided accommodation. The evaluation of books and accounts will also be conducted relating to employment matters, along with private interviews with staff members.

3. Based on Code 4.1, the manufacturers must follow the local and national laws, rules and regulations while operating. Failure to do so will result in a severe penalty and a breach in the Code of Conduct, adding the firm to a name of violators which is publicly available.

3.2.5 Ethical Theories

In this situation, the ethical theories that can be applied on RBS Factory, are the Rule Utilitarianism theory, Virtue theory and the Duty and Rights theory.

The theory focuses on the broad impacts of rules in the framework of the rule-of-usage theory and not on the operations of RBS Factory as a company. The essential objective is to comply with the specific laws which benefit most people and encourage public welfare. Correct action generally has good results, whereas bad action has horrible repercussions. Therefore, by limiting working hours maximum to 48 hours a week, and with the possibility of overtime of 12 hour, RBS Factory should do everything right, and paying for additional time is legal. In order to prevent them from working consecutively, they must also offer at least a day off a week. This may not save the company time and money but does more since the health and safety of employees and the public are on the line.

RBS Factory must first of all be honest, equitable, not damaging to other people, and so on, according to the ethic of virtue, duties and rights. The ethics of life, prosperity, liberalisation and so on are correct. The Ethics of Virtue argues that the RBS Factory should be moral as a business, serve people, have good and good features, etc. RBS Factory should thus take into account the safety and safety of the public and set up a close procedure and apply a heavy penalty to employees who are unable to operate without a cable safety check on LOTOs (Lock Out Tag Out).

RBS Smoking staff should also be penalised in their rooms for their brutality and non-professional behaviour, which might have caused a fire in them. This will improve the consciousness of employees and help to keep a working atmosphere across the company. If you wish to smoke, you have to smoke in a smoking zone outside your rooms. RBS Factory must ensure safe, clean and healthy shelter for its employees. If rodents and insects have discovered the lodging polluted, the farmers should immediately evacuate the employees and move them to an improved, clean, healthy house. They must also replace all fans that have no covers on them. RBS Factory must prioritize this, instead of conducting immoral behaviour and hindering the facts just to save money and time.

3.3   Analysis & Discussion of the Situation

Management may have a long-term impact on staff, on the environment and on the community if it does not take appropriate actions.

The first question is about the workforce for more than 60 hours a week, 8% of employees 12 months in a row and the company has no work hours and rest days monitoring policy or system for the workforce. Unless the issue is addressed, employees' morals and motivation are weak as they work unbelievably exhausted and drained extra hours. This frenzy plan puts a great deal of strain on employees' mental and physical health and endangers public and Community security by causing carelessness, care, and much more.

The second difficulty concerns the health and safety of employees working on the power cording and maintenance of the plant without LOTO (Lock Out Tag Out) and extended power cables used for the storage of chemical waste. If this issue is not addressed, employees are gravely risking their lives. This issue might result in injuries and limb amputations. If a factory employee works without a LOTO, it is labelled as a serious infringement in public press conferences in accordance with OSHA rules and legislation. The name of the firm will also be put on a public database of the egregious criminals. There is also a heavy penalty for the firm. In addition, an extension power wiring used in the waste chemicals storage area could result in electricity.

The third concern is individuals working without formal authorization in an unidentified confined section of the pump. This runs against to municipal law. When the local inspection catches workers without permission, there may be harsh fines and a high penalty for the organizing firm. Manufacturers are required to seek work license from local authorities and only then are the employees permitted to work in the confined region.

The fourth concern was the sleeping room inspection in which smoking employees were found in 2 houses on their beds, fans in 3 dormitories placed in the kitchen without covers, mice and insects, and a male guardian found in the women's bedroom. The employees must be accused of negligence and unprofessional behavior, which may have contributed to a burning in the areas. This will improve the consciousness of employees and help to keep a working atmosphere across the company. If you wish to smoke, you have to smoke in a smoking zone outside your rooms. The manufacturers must offer a safe, clean and healthy accommodation for their staff. If rodents and insects have discovered the lodging polluted, the farmers should immediately evacuate the employees and move them to an improved, clean, healthy house. They should also replace all fans with no protection, as a hand may be caught unintentionally, causing a disastrous injury. As for the matter of the male warden in the women's sleeping quarters, local law proposes that the individual explain what he did in the women's sleeping quarters. Failure to do so may lead the company, as required by local laws and regulations, to seriously punish and levy a high cost on the warden.

CONCLUSION

One of the numerous examples throughout the globe that question the way production works is detailed in this case study. The scenario There is nothing universal correct about the dilemma of certain ethics and it relies always on culture, because it's improper to have a males warden in a female dormitory in this situation, but it should be ok in many nations. Ethics like relativism, utilitarianism, responsibility and right ethics, virtue ethics, all engineers and employees ought to adhere to as they provide a wide notion of what sort of activity they ought to carry out.

Knowledge of professional norms of behaviors and where and when will assist the person to manage such decisions more readily over the long run. Therefore, this project was established to provide students the experience and technical skills they need to be based on, while still taking ethical values into account.

Disney's behavioral code, BEMs, WFEO and ethical theories have studied the situation. In each category, several solutions were offered. It may therefore be argued that the task has overarching targets.

REFERENCES

- Yumpu.com. 2021. Code of Conduct - English 2007 - The Walt Disney Company. [online] Available at: <https://www.yumpu.com/en/document/read/50473595/code-of-conduct-english-2007-the-walt-disney-company> [Accessed 3 September 2021].

- Mansfield, A., 2020. Why Ethics Are So Important For Engineers. [online] Blog.v-hr.com. Available at: <https://blog.v-hr.com/blog/why-ethics-are-so-important-for-engineers> [Accessed 27 July 2020].

- NJSPE. 2020. The Importance Of Ethics For Professional Engineers | NJSPE. [online] Available at: <https://njspe.org/2018/05/17/ethics-professional-engineers/#:~:text=The%20preamble%20to%20the%20NJSPE,much%20more%20than%20preventing%20illegal> [Accessed 27 July 2020].

- Tutorialspoint.com. 2020. Engineering Ethics - Ethical Theories - Tutorialspoint. [online] Available at: <https://www.tutorialspoint.com/engineering_ethics/engineering_ethical_theories.htm> [Accessed 23 August 2020].'

- Bem.org.my. 2015. Board of Engineers Malaysia. [online] Available at: <http://bem.org.my/web/guest/registration-of-engineers-act-1967-revised-2015-> [Accessed 27 July 2020].

- BIELEFELDT, A. (2018). Professional Social Responsibility in Engineering. *IntechOpen*. 3. pp. 1-21.

BEI GRIN MACHT SICH IHR WISSEN BEZAHLT

- Wir veröffentlichen Ihre Hausarbeit,
  Bachelor- und Masterarbeit

- Ihr eigenes eBook und Buch -
  weltweit in allen wichtigen Shops

- Verdienen Sie an jedem Verkauf

Jetzt bei www.GRIN.com hochladen
und kostenlos publizieren